MOSES
AND
THE VERY SPECIAL BASKET

by Sunny Griffin

Illustrated by Linda Welty

DID YOU KNOW...

Long ago there was a wicked king who didn't like any of the Israelites especially the baby boys?

DID YOU KNOW...
Moses' mother knew God would help save her baby boy from this wicked king?

DID YOU KNOW...
Miriam, Moses' big
sister loved her
little baby brother
very much?

DID YOU KNOW...
Moses' mother made
a very special basket
that would float
on the water?

DID YOU KNOW...
She hid Moses
in the very special
basket on the
river where Miriam
could watch it?

DID YOU KNOW…
When the King's
daughter and
her maid servants
came to the
river to bathe,
they found the very
special basket?

DID YOU KNOW...
A maid servant took
the very special
basket out of the
water and handed it
to the Princess?

DID YOU KNOW...
The Princess took
baby Moses out of
the very special basket
and hugged him
in her arms?

DID YOU KNOW...
Miriam rushed
over to the
Princess and told her
about a nurse for
the baby?

DID YOU KNOW...
The nurse Miriam
brought to the
Princess was Moses'
very own mother?

DID YOU KNOW...
The Princess loved
baby Moses and
raised him in the
palace as her
own son?

DID YOU KNOW...
Moses' mother thanked God every day for letting the King's daughter be the one to find her very special basket?

Moses grew up and trusted God just like his mother had done when he was a baby!